The Ultimate Air Fryer cookbook

Quick and easy recipes to begin a new journey. Lose weight while having fun cooking amazing low fat dishes

Linda Thompson

Table of Contents

Introduction

The Air fryer oven is an easy way to cook delicious healthy meals. It's the perfect appliance for the busy, on-the-go lifestyle. The Air Fryer oven does all the work. In a short amount of time, the Air fryer will showcase a perfectly fried chicken, steak, fish, or wings. The Air fryer oven is also suitable for baking too. You can now bake cakes, pies, and bread that are softer and less greasy when baking.

The Air Fryer has numerous advantages. It's non-stick, BPA-free, easy to clean, and easy to store. See how this Air Fryer does the work for you! It delivers your favorite fried recipes with 65 percent less fat. You can prepare food up to three times faster than in a traditional oven or on the stove. It helps maintain the nutritional content because, in a typical fryer, food is cooked at excessively high temperatures that can destroy nutrients like vitamins and minerals. When your food is prepared in an Air Fryer, it is only cooked to the safe temperatures appropriate for your health and the food. You can prepare healthy meals with less work, more control, and healthier results. It's the most efficient way to cook.

The Air Fryer will substitute these fats with a hot airflow, allowing it to have a crispy and delicious crust. You can control how crispy the crust of your food you want via the controls. You can cook at lower temperatures that are safe for your health, or you can go up to 250 degrees for more crispy goodness. It's easy to cook healthy food with less damage to its nutritional content. It is designed to cook healthier food that tastes better than food cooked in a traditional oil fryer. Cooking healthy food at an exact temperature is easy because every Air Fryer component is perfectly combined. All of your food feels the heat and is cooked evenly.

CHAPTER 1:

Breakfast and Brunch Recipes

1. Avocado Flautas

Preparation Time: 10 minutes

Cooking Time: 24 minutes

Servings: 8

Ingredients:

- 1 tbsp. butter Eight eggs, beaten

- ½ tsp. salt ¼ tsp. pepper

- 1 ½ tsp. cumin 1 tsp. chili powder

- Eight fajita-size tortillas

- 4 oz. cream cheese softened

- Eight slices of cooked bacon

Avocado Crème:

- Two small avocados

- ½ cup sour cream

- One lime, juiced

- ½ tsp. salt

- ¼ tsp. pepper

Directions:

1. In a skillet, melt butter and stir in eggs, salt, cumin, pepper, and chili powder, then stir cook for 4 minutes. Spread all the tortillas and top them with cream cheese and bacon. Then divide the egg scramble on top and finally add cheese.

2. Roll the tortillas to seal the filling inside. Place four rolls in the Air Fryer basket. Set the Air Fryer basket inside the Air Fryer toaster oven and close the lid. Select the Air Fry mode at 400 degrees F temperature for 12 minutes.

3. Cook the remaining tortilla rolls in the same manner. Meanwhile, blend avocado crème ingredients in a blender then serve with warm flautas.

Nutrition:

Calories: 212 Protein: 17.3g

Carbs: 14.6g

Fat: 11.8g

2. Cheese Sandwiches

Preparation Time: 10 minutes

Cooking Time: 10 minutes

Servings: 2

Ingredients:

- One egg

- 3 tbsp. Half and half cream

- ¼ tsp. vanilla extract

- Two slices sourdough, white or multigrain bread

- 2½ oz. sliced Swiss cheese

- 2 oz. sliced deli ham

- 2 oz. sliced deli turkey

- 1 tsp. butter, melted

- Powdered sugar

- Raspberry jam for serving

Directions:

1. Beat egg with half and half cream and vanilla extract in a bowl.

2. Place one bread slice on the working surface and top it with ham and turkey slices and Swiss cheese.

3. Place the other bread slice on top, then dip the sandwich in the egg mixture, then place it in a suitable baking tray lined with butter.

4. Set the baking tray inside the Air Fryer toaster oven and close the lid. Select the Air Fry mode at 350 degrees F temperature for 10 minutes.

5. Flip the sandwich and continue cooking for 8 minutes.

6. Slice and serve.

Nutrition:

Calories: 412

Protein: 18.9g

Carbs: 43.8g

Fat: 24.8g

3. Sausage Cheese Wraps

Preparation Time: 10 minutes **Cooking Time:** 3 minutes

Servings: 8

Ingredients:

- Eight sausages Two pieces of American cheese, shredded

- 8-count refrigerated crescent roll dough

Directions:

1. Roll out and top each crescent roll with cheese and one sausage.

2. Fold both the crescent sheet's top and bottom edges to cover the sausage and roll it around the sausage.

3. Place four rolls in the Air Fryer basket and spray them with cooking oil. Set the Air Fryer basket inside the Air Fryer toaster oven and close the lid.

4. Select the Air Fry mode at 380 degrees F temperature for 3 minutes. Cook the remaining rolls in the same manner. Serve fresh.

Nutrition:

Calories: 296 Protein: 34.2g Carbs: 17g

Fat: 22.1g

4. Bacon, Mushroom & Tomato Frittata

Preparation Time: 15 minutes

Cooking Time: 16 minutes

Servings: 2

Ingredients:

- One cooked bacon slice, chopped
- Six cherry tomatoes halved
- Six fresh mushrooms, sliced
- Salt and ground black pepper, as required
- Three eggs
- 1 tbsp. fresh parsley, chopped
- ¼ cup Parmesan cheese, grated

Directions:

1. In a prepared baking pan, add the bacon, tomatoes, mushrooms, salt, and black pepper and mix well.
2. Select the "Air Fry" mode.
3. Press the Time button and set the cooking time to 16 minutes.
4. Now set the temperature at 320 degrees F.
5. Press the "Start/Pause" button to start.
6. When it is preheated, open the lid.

7. Arrange pan over the "Wire Rack" and insert in the oven.

8. Meanwhile, in a bowl, add the eggs and beat well.

9. Add the parsley and cheese and mix well.

10. After 6 minutes of cooking, top the bacon mixture with egg mixture evenly.

11. Cut into equal-sized wedges and serve.

Nutrition:

Calories 228

Fat 15.5 g

Cholesterol 270 mg

Total Carbs 3.5 g

Fiber 0.9 g

Sugar 2.1 g

Protein 19.8 g

5. Cinnamon Buns

Preparation Time: 5 minutes

Cooking Time: 15 minutes

Servings: 2

Ingredients

- 8 oz. container crescent rolls, refrigerated

- 1 tbsp. ground cinnamon

- 2 oz. raisins

- 1/3 cup butter

- 2 tbsp. sugar, granulated

- 1/3 cup pecans, chopped

- cooking spray (olive oil)

- Maple syrup – 2 tbsp.

- 1/3 cup brown sugar

Directions

1. In a saucepan, dissolve the butter completely. Transfer to a dish and blend the maple syrup and brown sugar.

2. Layer one 8-inch pan with the olive oil spray.

3. Distribute the sugar into the pan and empty the raisins and pecans inside, stirring to incorporate.

4. In a glass dish, whisk the sugar and ground cinnamon.

5. Open the can of crescent rolls and place it on a cutting board.

6. Slice the entire log of dough into eight individual pieces.

7. Cover the top and bottom of the dough pieces in cinnamon and sugar, and transfer the pan to the air fryer.

8. Adjust the settings to air crisp at 345° F for 5 minutes.

9. Turn over the individual buns and steam for another 5 minutes.

10. Take the pan out and move the buns to a serving plate.

11. Drizzle the remaining sugar liquid on the buns and serve immediately.

Nutrition:

Energy (calories): 1012 kcal

Protein: 14.09 g

Fat: 46.6 g

Carbohydrates: 141.75 g

6. Egg and Cheese Veggie Cups

Preparation Time: 10 minutes

Cooking Time: 35minutes

Servings: 2

Ingredients

- cooking spray (olive oil)

- large eggs - 4

- 1/4 tsp. salt

- 2 oz. half & half

- cheddar cheese – 8oz, shredded

- 3 tsp. chopped cilantro

- 1/8 tsp. pepper

Directions

1. Set the air fryer to the temperature of 300° F to heat.

2. Liberally spray four glasses or ceramic ramekin dishes.

3. In a glass dish, blend the half & half, salt, cilantro, eggs, pepper, and 4 oz. of the shredded cheese until combined.

4. Evenly distribute the mixture to the greased dishes.

5. Move the dishes to the basket in the air fryer for 12 minutes.

6. Once the time has passed, sprinkle the remaining 4 oz. of shredded cheese on top of each dish.

7. Adjust the temperature to 400° F and broil for an additional 2 minutes.

8. Serve immediately and enjoy!

Nutrition:

Energy (calories): 272 kcal

Protein: 18.71 g

Fat: 14.99 g

Carbohydrates: 15.6 g

CHAPTER 2:

Snacks, Appetizers, and Sides

7. Parsnips and Thyme Fries

Preparation Time: 5 minutes

Cooking Time: 15 minutes

Servings: 4

Ingredients:

- Four parsnips, cut into medium sticks

- Four carrots, cut into medium sticks

- Salt and black pepper to taste

- 2 tbsps. thyme, chopped

- 2 tbsps. olive oil

- ½ tsp. onion powder

Directions:

1. In a bowl, mix all ingredients and toss.

2. Transfer the fries to your air fryer's basket and cook at 350 degrees F for 15 minutes.

3. Divide between plates and serve as a side dish.

Nutrition:

Calories 160

Fat 3g

Fiber 4g

Carbs 7g

Protein 3g

8. Pepper Tomatoes Mix

Preparation Time: 5 minutes

Cooking Time: 15 minutes

Servings: 6

Ingredients:

- 15 ounces mushrooms, roughly sliced

- One red onion, chopped

- Salt and black pepper to taste

- ½ tsp. nutmeg, ground

- 2 tbsps. olive oil

- 6 ounces canned tomatoes, chopped

Directions:

1. Place all ingredients in a pan that fits your air fryer and mix well.

2. Put the pan in the fryer and cook at 380 degrees F for 15 minutes.

3. Divide the mix between plates and serve as a side dish.

Nutrition:

Calories 202 Fat 6g Fiber 1g Carbs 16g

Protein 4g

9. Yellow Squash and Zucchini Mix

Preparation Time: 10 minutes

Cooking Time: 35 minutes

Servings: 4

Ingredients:

- 5 tsp. olive oil

- 1 pound zucchinis, sliced

- One yellow squash, halved, deseeded, and cut into chunks

- Salt and white pepper to taste

- 1 tbsp. cilantro, chopped

Directions:

1. In a prepared bowl, mix all the ingredients, toss well, and transfer them to your air fryer's basket.

2. Cook for 35 minutes at 400 degrees.

3. Divide everything between plates and serve as a side dish.

Nutrition:

Calories 200 Fat 4g Fiber 1g

Carbs 15g

Protein 4g

10. Cheesy Mushroom Salad

Preparation Time: 5 minutes **Cooking Time:** 15 minutes

Servings: 3

Ingredients:

- Ten large mushrooms halved 1 tbsp. mixed herbs, dried

- 1 tbsp. cheddar cheese, grated

- 1 tbsp. mozzarella cheese, grated

- A drizzle of olive oil

- 2 tsp. parsley flakes

- Salt and black pepper to taste

Directions:

1. Use the oil to grease a pan that fits your air fryer.

2. Add all other ingredients and toss.

3. Place the pan in the fryer and cook at 380 degrees F for 15 minutes.

4. Divide between plates and serve as a side dish.

Nutrition:

Calories 161 Fat 7g Fiber 1g Carbs 12g

Protein 6 g

11. Hearty Baby Bok Choy

Preparation Time: 5 minutes

Cooking Time: 6 minutes

Servings: 4

Ingredients

- Four bunch baby bok choy
- 1 tsp. garlic powder

Directions:

1. Preheat your Air Fryer 350 degrees F.

2. Prepare your baby bok choy by slicing off the bottom and separating the leaves, rinse well.

3. Transfer to your Air Fryer and drizzle olive oil, sprinkle garlic powder.

4. Cook for 6 minutes, making sure to shake about halfway through until golden brown.

5. Serve and enjoy.

Nutrition:

Calories: 58 Fat: 2g

Carbohydrates: 5g

Protein: 1g

12. Tangy Broccoli Asparagus

Preparation Time: 5 minutes

Cooking Time: 20 minutes

Servings: 4

Ingredients

- ½ pound asparagus, cut into one and ½ inch pieces

- ½ pound broccoli, cut into one and ½ inch pieces

- 2 tbsps. peanut oil

- Salt and pepper to taste

- ½ cup vegetable broth

- 2 tbsps. apple cider vinegar

Directions:

1. Preheat your Air Fryer 380 degrees F.

2. Place vegetables in a single layer, grease lightly.

3. Drizzle peanut oil over vegetables.

4. Season with salt and pepper.

5. Transfer to the cooking basket and cook for 15 minutes, making sure to shake about halfway through.

6. Add ½ cup broth to the saucepan and bring to a boil. Add vinegar and then cook for 5-7 minutes until sauce is reduced.

7. Spoon over veggies and serve.

8. Enjoy.

Nutrition:

Calories: 144

Fat: 10g

Carbohydrates: 6g

Protein: 10g

CHAPTER 3:

Vegetable Recipes

13. Spaghetti Squash Tots

Preparation Time: 5 minutes

Cooking Time: 15 minutes

Servings: 810

Ingredients:

- ¼tsp. Pepper

- ½tsp. Salt

- One thinly sliced scallion

- One spaghetti squash

Directions:

1. Wash and then cut the squash in half lengthwise. Scrape out the seeds.

2. With a fork, remove spaghetti meat by strands and throw out skins.

3. In a clean towel, toss in squash and wring out as much moisture as possible. Place in a bowl and with a knife, slice it a few times to cut up smaller.

4. Add pepper, salt, and scallions to squash and mix well.

5. Create "tot" shapes with your hands and place them in an air fryer. Spray with olive oil.

6. Cook 15 minutes at 350 degrees until golden and crispy.

Nutrition:

Calories: 231

Fat: 18g

Protein: 5g

Sugar: 0g

14. Cinnamon Butternut Squash Fries

Preparation Time: 10 minutes

Cooking Time: 10 minutes

Servings: 2

Ingredients:

- One pinch of salt

- 1 tbsp. Powdered unprocessed sugar

- ½tsp. Nutmeg

- 2 tsp. Cinnamon

- 1 tbsp. Coconut oil

- 10 ounces precut butternut squash fries

Directions:

1. In a plastic bag, pour in all ingredients. Coat fries with other components till coated and sugar is dissolved.

2. Spread coated fries into a single layer in the air fryer. Cook 10 minutes at 390 degrees until crispy.

Nutrition:

Calories: 175 Fat: 8g

Protein: 1g

Sugar: 5g

15. Paprika Tomatoes

Preparation Time: 10 minutes

Cooking Time: 15 minutes

Servings: 4

Ingredients:

- 1pound cherry tomatoes halved

- 1 tbsp. sweet paprika

- 2 tbsps. olive oil

- Two garlic cloves, minced

- 1 tbsp. lime juice

- 1 tbsp. chives, chopped

Directions:

1. In your air fryer's basket, combine the tomatoes with the paprika and the other ingredients, toss and cook at a temperature of 370 degrees f for 15 minutes.

2. Divide between plates and serve.

Nutrition:

Calories 131 Fat 4g

Fiber 7g Carbohydrates 10g

Protein 8g

16. Avocado And Tomato Salad

Preparation Time: 10 minutes

Cooking Time: 12 minutes

Servings: 4

Ingredients:

- 1pound tomatoes, cut into wedges

- Two avocados, peeled, pitted, and sliced

- 2 tbsps. avocado oil

- One red onion, sliced

- 1 tbsp. balsamic vinegar

- Salt and black pepper to the taste

- 1 tbsp. cilantro, chopped

Directions:

1. In your air fryer, combine the tomatoes with the avocados and the other ingredients, toss and cook at 360 degrees f for 12 minutes.

2. Divide between plates and serve.

Nutrition:

Calories 144 Fat 7g Fiber 5g Carbohydrates 8g

Protein 6g

17. Sesame Broccoli Mix

Preparation Time: 5 minutes

Cooking Time: 14 minutes

Servings: 4

Ingredients:

- 1pound broccoli florets

- 1 tbsp. sesame oil

- 1 tsp. sesame seeds, toasted

- One red onion, sliced

- 1 tbsp. lime juice

- 1 tsp. chili powder

- Salt and black pepper to the taste

Directions:

1. In your air fryer, combine the broccoli with the oil, sesame seeds, and the other ingredients, toss and cook at 380 degrees f for 14 minutes.

2. Divide between plates and serve.

Nutrition:

Calories 141 Fat 3g Fiber 4g Carbohydrates 4g

Protein 2g

18. Cabbage Sauté

Preparation Time: 5 minutes

Cooking Time: 15 minutes

Servings: 4

Ingredients:

- 1pound red cabbage, shredded

- 1 tbsp. balsamic vinegar

- Two red onions, sliced

- 1 tbsp. olive oil

- 1 tbsp. dill, chopped

- Salt and black pepper to the taste

Directions:

1. Heat air fryer with oil at 380 degrees f, add the cabbage, onions, and the other ingredients, toss and cook for 15 minutes.

2. Divide between plates and serve.

Nutrition:

Calories 100 Fat 4g Fiber 2g

Carbohydrates 7g

Protein 2g

CHAPTER 4:

Poultry Recipes

19. Turkish Chicken Kebabs

Preparation Time: 15 minutes

Cooking Time: 15 minutes

Servings: 4

Ingredients:

- ¼ cup plain Greek yogurt

- 1 tbsp. minced garlic

- 1 tbsp. tomato paste

- 1 tbsp. fresh lemon juice

- 1 tbsp. vegetable oil

- 1 tsp. kosher salt

- 1 tsp. ground cumin

- 1 tsp. sweet Hungarian paprika

- ½ tsp. ground cinnamon

- ½ tsp. black pepper

- ½ tsp. cayenne pepper

- 1 pound or (454 g) boneless, skinless chicken thighs, quartered crosswise

Directions:

1. In a large bowl, combine the yogurt, garlic, tomato paste, lemon juice, vegetable oil, salt, cumin, paprika, cinnamon, black pepper, and cayenne. Stir until the spices are blended into the yogurt.

2. Add the chicken to the bowl and toss until well coated. Marinate for 30 minutes, then cover or refrigerate for up to 24 hours.

3. Press Start/Cancel. Preheat the air fryer oven to 375°F (191°C).

4. Arrange the chicken in a single layer in the fry basket. Insert the fry basket at mid position. Select Air Fry, Convection, and set time to 10 minutes. Turn the chicken and air fry for 5 minutes more. Use a meat thermometer to ensure the chicken has reached an internal temperature of 165°F (74°C).

5. Serve warm.

Nutrition:

Energy (calories): 240 kcal

Protein: 11.09 g

Fat: 10.14 g

Carbohydrates: 26.58 g

20. Hawaiian Tropical Chicken

Preparation Time: 10 minutes

Cooking Time: 15 minutes

Servings: 4

Ingredients:

- Four boneless, skinless chicken thighs (1½ pounds / 680 g)

- 1 (8-ounce / 227-g) can pineapple chunks in juice, drained, ¼ cup juice reserved

- ¼ cup soy sauce

- ¼ cup sugar

- 2 tbsps. ketchup

- 1 tbsp. minced fresh ginger

- 1 tbsp. minced garlic

- ¼ cup chopped scallions

Directions:

1. Use a fork to pierce the chicken all over to allow the marinade to penetrate better. Place the chicken in a prepared large bowl or large resealable plastic bag.

2. Set the drained pineapple chunks aside. In a small microwave-safe bowl, combine the pineapple juice, soy sauce, sugar,

ketchup, ginger, and garlic. Pour half the sauce over the chicken; toss to coat. Reserve the remaining sauce. Marinate the chicken for 30 minutes, then cover or refrigerate for up to 24 hours.

3. Press Start/Cancel. Preheat the air fryer oven, set the temperature to 350°F (177°C).

4. Place the chicken in the fry basket, discarding marinade. Insert at a low position. Select Bake, Convection, and set time to 15 minutes, turning halfway through the cooking time.

5. Meanwhile, microwave the reserved sauce on high for 45 to 60 seconds, stirring every 15 seconds, until the sauce has the consistency of a thick glaze.

6. Using a meat thermometer at the end of cooking time to ensure that the chicken has reached an internal temperature of 165F (74C).

7. Transfer the chicken to a serving platter. Pour the sauce over the chicken. Garnish with the pineapple chunks and scallions before serving.

Nutrition: Energy (calories): 123 kcal Protein: 1.76 g Fat: 2.98 g Carbohydrates: 23.73 g

21. Yellow Curry Chicken Thighs with Peanuts

Preparation Time: 10 minutes

Cooking Time: 20 minutes

Servings: 6

Ingredients:

- ½ cup unsweetened full-fat coconut milk

- 2 tbsps. yellow curry paste

- 1 tbsp. minced fresh ginger

- 1 tbsp. minced garlic

- 1 tsp. kosher salt

- 1 pound or (454 g) boneless, skinless chicken thighs, halved crosswise

- 2 tbsps. chopped peanuts

Directions:

1. In a large bowl, stir together the coconut milk, curry paste, ginger, garlic, and salt until well blended. Add the chicken; toss well to coat. Marinate for 30 minutes and cover or refrigerate for up to 24 hours.

2. Press Start/Cancel. Preheat the air fryer oven to 375°F (191°C).

3. Place the chicken (along with marinade) in a baking pan. Place the pan in the fry basket. Insert at a low position.

4. Select Bake, Convection, and set time to 20 minutes, turning the chicken halfway through the cooking time. Use a meat thermometer to ensure the chicken has reached an internal temperature of 165°F (74°C).

5. Sprinkle with the chopped peanuts over the chicken and serve.

Nutrition:

Energy (calories): 218 kcal

Protein: 9.43 g

Fat: 11.42 g

Carbohydrates: 20.86 g

22. Chicken Burgers with Ham and Cheese

Preparation Time: 12 minutes

Cooking Time: 15 minutes

Servings: 4

Ingredients:

- $^1/3$ cup soft bread crumbs

- 3 tbsps. milk

- One egg, beaten

- ½ tsp. dried thyme

- Pinch salt

- Freshly ground black pepper to taste

- 1¼ pounds (567 g) ground chicken

- ¼ cup finely chopped ham

- $^1/3$ cup grated Havarti cheese

- Olive oil for misting

Directions:

1. Press Start/Cancel. Preheat the air fryer oven temperature to 350°F (177°C).

2. In a prepared medium bowl, combine the bread crumbs, milk, egg, thyme, salt, and pepper. Add the chicken and mix gently but thoroughly with clean hands.

3. Form the chicken into eight thin patties and place on waxed paper.

4. Top four of the patties with the ham and cheese. Top with the remaining four patties and gently press the edges together to seal, so the ham and cheese mixture is in the middle of the burger.

5. Place the burgers in the basket and mist with olive oil. Insert at a low position. Select Bake, Convection, and set time to 15 minutes, or until the chicken is thoroughly cooked to 165°F (74°C) as measured with a meat thermometer.

6. Serve immediately.

Nutrition:

Energy (calories): 247 kcal

Protein: 23.47 g

Fat: 14.34 g

Carbohydrates: 5.78 g

23. Chicken Satay with Peanut Sauce

Preparation Time: 12 minutes

Cooking Time: 8 minutes

Servings: 4

Ingredients:

- ½ cup crunchy peanut butter

- ¹/3 cup chicken broth

- 3 tbsps. low-sodium soy sauce

- 2 tbsps. lemon juice

- Two cloves garlic, minced

- 2 tbsps. olive oil

- 1 tsp. curry powder

- 1 pound (454 g) chicken tenders

Directions:

1. Press Start/Cancel. Preheat the air fryer oven to 390°F (199°C).

2. In a prepared medium bowl, combine the peanut butter, chicken broth, soy sauce, lemon juice, garlic, olive oil, and curry powder, and mix well with a wire whisk until smooth.

Remove 2 tbsps of this mixture to a small bowl. Put the remaining sauce into a serving bowl and set aside.

3. Add the chicken tenders to the bowl with the 2 tbsps sauce and stir to coat. Let stand for a few minutes to marinate, and then run a bamboo skewer through each chicken tender lengthwise.

4. Put the chicken in the fry basket and insert the fry basket at mid position. Select Air Fry, Convection, and set time to 8 minutes, or until the chicken reaches 165°F (74°C) on a meat thermometer. Serve the chicken with the reserved sauce.

Nutrition:

Calories: 765 kcal

Protein: 66.97 g

Fat: 39.44 g

Carbohydrates: 36.31 g

24. Fried Buffalo Chicken Taquitos

Preparation Time: 15 minutes

Cooking Time: 8 minutes

Servings: 6

Ingredients:

- 8 ounces (227 g) fat-free cream cheese, softened

- 1/8 cup Buffalo sauce

- cups shredded cooked chicken

- 12 (7-inch) low-carb flour tortillas

- Olive oil spray

Directions:

1. Press Start/Cancel. Preheat the air fryer oven to 360°F (182°C). Spray the fry basket lightly with olive oil spray.

2. In a prepared large bowl, mix the cream cheese and Buffalo sauce until well combined. Add the chicken and stir until combined.

3. Place the tortillas on a clean workspace. Spoon 2 to 3 tbsps of the chicken mixture in a thin line down the center of each tortilla. Roll up the tortillas.

4. Place the tortillas in the fry basket, seam-side down. Spray each tortilla lightly with olive oil spray. You may need to cook the taquitos in batches.

5. Insert the fry basket at mid position. Select Air Fry, Convection, and set time to 8 minutes, or until golden brown. Serve hot.

Nutrition:

Energy (calories): 135 kcal

Protein: 9.78 g

Fat: 8.01 g

Carbohydrates: 5.42 g

25. Celery Chicken

Preparation Time: 10 minutes

Cooking Time: 14 minutes

Servings: 4

Ingredients:

- ½ cup soy sauce

- 2 tbsps. hoisin sauce

- 4 tsp. minced garlic

- 1 tsp. freshly ground black pepper

- Eight boneless, skinless chicken tenderloins

- 1 cup chopped celery

- One medium red bell pepper, diced

- Olive oil spray

Directions:

1. Press Start/Cancel. Preheat the air fryer oven to 375°F (191°C). Spray the fry basket lightly with olive oil spray.

2. In a prepared large bowl, mix the soy sauce, hoisin sauce, garlic, and black pepper to make a marinade. Add the chicken, celery, and bell pepper and toss to coat.

3. Shake the excess marinade off the chicken, place it and the vegetables in the fry basket, and lightly spray with olive oil spray. You may have to cook them in batches. Reserve the remaining marinade.

4. Insert the fry basket at mid position. Select Air Fry, Convection, and set time to 8 minutes. Switch over the chicken and brush some of the remaining marinades with it. Air fry for an additional 6 minutes, or until the chicken reaches an internal temperature of at least 165°F (74°C). Serve.

Nutrition:

Energy (calories): 123 kcal

Protein: 3.11 g

Fat: 6.12 g

Carbohydrates: 14.19 g

CHAPTER 5:

Beef Recipes

26. Beef Rib Eye Steak

Preparation Time: 5 minutes

Cooking Time: 20 minutes

Servings: 4

Ingredients

- 4 (8-ounce) ribeye steaks

- 1 tbsp. McCormick Grill Mates Montreal Steak Seasoning

- Salt

- Pepper

Directions:

1. Season the steaks with the steak seasoning and salt and pepper to taste. Place two steaks in the Air Fryer Oven. You can use an accessory grill pan, a layer rack, or the air fryer basket.

2. Cook for 4 minutes. Open the air fryer and flip the steaks.

3. Cook for an additional 4 to 5 minutes. Check for doneness to determine how much additional cook time is a need. Remove the cooked steaks from the Air Fryer Oven, and then repeat for the remaining two steaks. Cool before serving.

Nutrition:

Calories: 293

Fat: 22g

Protein: 23g

Fiber: 0g

27. Air Fryer Roast Beef

Preparation Time: 5 minutes

Cooking Time: 45 minutes

Servings: 6

Ingredients

- Roast beef
- 1 tbsp. olive oil
- Seasonings of choice

Directions:

1. Ensure your Air Fryer Oven is preheated to 160 degrees.

2. Place roast in the bowl and toss with olive oil and desired seasonings.

3. Put seasoned roast into the air fryer.

4. Set temperature to 160°F, and set time to 30 minutes, and cook 30 minutes.

5. Turn roast when the timer sounds and cook for another 15 minutes.

Nutrition:

Calories: 267 Fat: 8g Protein: 21g

Sugar: 1g

28. Beef Korma

Preparation Time: 10 minutes

Cooking Time: 20 minutes

Servings: 6

Ingredients

- ½ cup yogurt

- 1 kg (2.2 lbs.) boneless beef steak, cut in chunks

- 1 tbsp. curry powder

- 1 tbsp. olive oil

- One onion, chopped

- 3 cloves garlic, minced

- One tomato, diced

- ½ cup frozen baby peas, thawed

Directions:

1. In a medium bowl, combine the steak, yogurt, and curry powder. Stir and set aside.

2. In a 6-inch metal bowl, combine the olive oil, onion, and garlic.

3. Cook for 3 to 4 minutes or until crisp and tender.

4. Add the steak along with the yogurt and the diced tomato. Cook for 12 to 13 minutes or until the steak is almost tender.

5. Stir in the peas and cook for 2 to 3 minutes or until hot.

Nutrition:

Calories: 289

Fat: 11g

Protein: 38g

Fiber: 2g

29. Herb and Onion Beef Roast

Preparation Time: 10 minutes

Cooking Time: 45 minutes

Servings: 4

Ingredients

- 1 ½ pound beef eye round roast

- 1 tbsp. olive oil

- Sea salt and ground black pepper to taste

- One onion, sliced

- One rosemary sprig

- One thyme sprig

Directions

1. Toss the beef with olive oil, salt, and black pepper; place the beef in the Air Fryer cooking basket.

2. Cook the beef eye round roast at 390 degrees F for 45 minutes, turning it over halfway through the cooking time.

3. Top the beef with onion, rosemary, and thyme. Continue to cook for an additional 10 minutes.

Nutrition: Calories 268 Fat 13.6g Carbs 1.2g Protein35.2g Sugars0.6g Fiber0.2g

30. Easy Fried Porterhouse

Preparation Time: 5 minutes **Cooking Time:** 10 minutes

Servings: 4

Ingredients

- 1 ½ pound Porterhouse steak 1 tbsp. olive oil

- Kosher salt and ground black pepper to taste

- 1/2 tsp. cayenne pepper 1 tsp. dried parsley

- 1 tsp. dried oregano 1/2 tsp. dried basil

- 6 tbsps. butter

- 4 garlic cloves, minced

Directions

1. Toss the steak with the remaining ingredients; place the steak in the Air Fryer cooking basket.

2. Cook the steak at 400 degrees F for 12 minutes, turning it over halfway through the cooking time.

3. Bon appétit!

Nutrition:

Calories326 Fat19.6g Carbs1.9g

Protein35.6g Sugars0.6g

Fiber0.4g

31. Restaurant-Style Beef Burgers

Preparation Time: 5 minutes **Cooking Time:** 15 minutes

Servings: 3

Ingredients

- 3/4 pound ground beef 2 cloves garlic, minced

- One small onion, chopped

- Kosher salt and ground black pepper to taste

- 3 hamburger buns

Directions

1. Mix the beef, garlic, onion, salt, and black pepper until everything is well combined. Form the mixture into three patties.

2. Cook the burgers at 380 degrees F for about 15 minutes or until cooked through; make sure to turn them over halfway through the cooking time.

3. Serve your burgers on the prepared buns and enjoy!

Nutrition:

Calories 392 Fat 16.6g

Carbs 32.3g Protein 28.2g

Sugars 5.3g Fiber 1.8g

CHAPTER 6:

Pork and Lamb Recipes

32. Lemony Lamb Chops

Preparation Time: 10 minutes

Cooking Time: 25 minutes

Servings: 2

Ingredients

- Two medium lamb chops

- ¼ cup lemon juice

Directions:

1. Liberally rub the lamb chops with lemon juice.

2. Place the lemony chops in the air fryer basket.

3. Press the "Power Button" of the Air Fry Oven and turn the dial to select the "Air Fry" mode.

4. Press the Time button and again turn the dial to set the cooking time to 25 minutes.

5. Now push the Temp button and rotate the dial to set the temperature at 350 degrees F.

6. Once preheated, place the Air fryer basket in the oven and close its lid.

7. Flip the chops when cooked halfway through, then resume cooking.

8. Serve warm.

Nutrition:

Calories 529

Fat 17 g

Cholesterol 65 mg

Carbs 55 g

Fiber 6 g

Protein 41g

33. Garlicky Rosemary Lamb Chops

Preparation Time: 10 minutes

Cooking Time: 10 minutes

Servings: 4

Ingredients

- Four lamb chops

- 2 tsp. olive oil

- 1 tsp. fresh rosemary

- Two garlic cloves, minced

- 2 tsp. garlic puree

- Salt & black pepper

Directions:

1. Place lamb chops in the air fryer basket.

2. Rub them with olive oil, rosemary, garlic, garlic puree, salt, and black pepper

3. Press the "Power Button" of the Air Fry Oven and turn the dial to select the "Air Fry" mode.

4. Press the Time button and again turn the dial to set the cooking time to 12 minutes.

5. Now push the Temp button and rotate the dial to set the temperature at 350 degrees F.

6. Once preheated, place the Air fryer basket in the oven and close its lid.

7. Flip the chops when cooked halfway through, then resume cooking.

8. Serve warm.

Nutrition:

Calories 297

Fat 14 g

Cholesterol 99 mg

Total Carbs 8 g

Fiber 1 g

Protein 32 g

34. Lamb Tomato Bake

Preparation Time: 10 minutes

Cooking Time: 35 minutes

Servings: 6

Ingredients

- 25 oz. potatoes, boiled

- 14 oz. lean lamb mince

- 1 tsp. cinnamon

- 23 oz. jar tomato pasta

Sauce

- 12 oz. white sauce

- 1 tbsp. olive oil

Directions:

1. Mash the potatoes in a bowl and stir in white sauce and cinnamon.

2. Sauté lamb mince with olive oil in a frying pan until brown.

3. Layer a casserole dish with tomato pasta sauce.

4. Top the sauce with lamb mince.

5. Spread the potato mash over the lamb in an even layer.

6. Press the "Power Button" of the Air Fry Oven and turn the dial to select the "Bake" mode.

7. Press the Time button and again turn the dial to set the cooking time to 35 minutes.

8. Now push the Temp button and rotate the dial to set the temperature at 350 degrees F.

9. Once preheated, place the casserole dish in the oven and close its lid.

10. Serve warm.

Nutrition:

Calories 352

Fat 14 g

Cholesterol 65 mg

Carbs 15.8 g

Fiber 0.2 g

Protein 26 g

35. Lamb Baked with Tomato Topping

Preparation Time: 10 minutes

Cooking Time: 100 minutes

Servings: 8

Ingredients

- Eight lamb shoulder chops, trimmed

- 1/4 cup plain flour

- 1 tbsp. olive oil

- One large brown onion, chopped

- Two garlic cloves, crushed

- Three medium carrots, peeled and diced

- 2 tbsps. tomato paste

- 2 1/2 cups beef stock

- Two dried bay leaves

- 1 cup frozen peas

- 3 cups potato gems

Directions:

1. Dust the lamb chops with flour and sear it in a pan layered with olive oil.

2. Sear the lamb chops for 4 minutes per side.

3. Transfer the chops to a baking tray.

4. Add onion, garlic, and carrot to the same pan.

5. Sauté for 5 minutes, then stir in tomato paste, stock, and all other ingredients.

6. Stir cook for 4 minutes, then pour this sauce over the chops.

7. Press the "Power Button" of the Air Fry Oven and turn the dial to select the "Bake" mode.

8. Press the Time button and turn the dial to set the cooking time to 1 hr. 30 minutes.

9. Now push the Temp button and rotate the dial to set the temperature at 350 degrees F.

10. When preheated, put the baking pan in the oven and close its lid.

11. Serve warm.

Nutrition:

Calories 388 Fat 8 g

Cholesterol 153mg

Carbs 8 g

Fiber 1 g

Protein 13 g

36. Lamb Potato Chips Baked

Preparation Time: 10 minutes

Cooking Time: 25 minutes

Servings: 4

Ingredients

- ½ lb. minced lamb

- 1 tbsp. parsley chopped

- 2 tsp. curry powder

- One pinch of salt and black pepper

- 1 lb. potato cooked, mashed

- 1 oz. cheese grated

- 1 ½ oz. potato chips crushed

Directions:

1. Mix lamb, curry powder, seasoning, and parsley.

2. Spread this lamb mixture in a casserole dish.

3. Top the lamb mixture with potato mash, cheese, and potato chips.

4. Press the "Power Button" of the Air Fry Oven and turn the dial to select the "Bake" mode.

5. Press the Time button and again turn the dial to set the cooking time to 20 minutes.

6. Now push the Temp button and rotate the dial to set the temperature at 350 degrees F.

7. Once preheated, place the casserole dish in the oven and close its lid.

8. Serve warm.

Nutrition:

Calories 301

Fat 15.8 g

Cholesterol 75 mg

Carbs 31.7 g

Fiber 0.3 g

Protein 28.2 g

CHAPTER 7:

Fish and Seafood Recipes

37. Cilantro-Lime Fried Shrimp

Preparation Time: 10 minutes

Cooking Time: 10 minutes

Servings: 4

Ingredients

- 2-pound raw shrimp, peeled and deveined with tails on or off (see Prep tip) ½ cup chopped fresh cilantro

- Juice of 1 lime

- One egg ½ cup all-purpose flour

- ¾ cup bread crumbs

- Salt Pepper

- Cooking oil

- ½ cup cocktail sauce (optional)

Directions:

1. Preparing the **Ingredients**. Place the shrimp in a plastic bag and add the cilantro and lime juice. Seal the bag. Shake to combine. Marinate in the refrigerator for 30 minutes. In a small bowl, beat the egg. In another small bowl, place the flour. Place the bread crumbs in a third small bowl, and season with salt and pepper to taste. Spray the air fryer rack/basket with cooking oil. Remove the shrimp from the plastic bag. Dip each in the flour, then the egg, and then the bread crumbs.

2. Air Frying. Place the shrimp in the Air fryer oven. It is okay to stack them. Spray the shrimp with cooking oil. Set temperature to 360°F. Cook for 4 minutes. Open the air fryer and flip the shrimp. I recommend flipping individually instead of shaking to keep the breading intact. Cook for another 4 minutes, or until crisp. Cool before serving. Serve with cocktail sauce if desired.

Nutrition:

Calories: 254 Fat: 4g

Protein: 29g

Fiber: 1g

38. Lemony Tuna

Preparation Time: 10 minutes

Cooking Time: 10 minutes

Servings: 4

Ingredients

- (6-ounce) cans water-packed plain tuna

- 2 tsp. Dijon mustard

- ½ cup breadcrumbs

- 1 tbsp. fresh lime juice

- 2 tbsps. fresh parsley, chopped

- One egg

- Chefman of hot sauce

- 4 tbsps. canola oil

- Salt

- freshly ground black pepper to taste

Directions:

1. Preparing the **Ingredients**. Drain out much of the canned tuna oil. In a bowl, add the fish, mustard, crumbs, citrus juice, parsley, and hot sauce and mix till well combined. Add a little canola oil if it seems too dry. Add egg, salt, and stir to

combine. Make the patties from the tuna mixture. Refrigerate the tuna patties for about 2 hours.

2. Air Frying. Preheat the air fryer oven, set the temperature to 355 degrees F. Cook for about 10-12 minutes.

Nutrition:

Energy (calories): 66 kcal

Protein: 2.41 g

Fat: 6.01 g

Carbohydrates: 0.84 g

39. Grilled Soy Salmon Fillets

Preparation Time: 5 minutes

Cooking Time: 8 minutes

Servings: 4

Ingredients

- Four salmon fillets

- 1/4 tsp. ground black pepper

- 1/2 tsp. cayenne pepper

- 1/2 tsp. salt

- 1 tsp. onion powder

- 1 tbsp. fresh lemon juice

- 1/2 cup soy sauce

- 1/2 cup water

- 1 tbsp. honey

- 2 tbsps. extra-virgin olive oil

Directions:

1. Preparing the **Ingredients**. Firstly, pat the salmon fillets dry using kitchen towels. Season the salmon with black pepper, cayenne pepper, salt, and onion powder. To make the marinade, combine lemon juice, soy sauce, water, honey, and

olive oil. Marinate the salmon for at least 2 hours in your refrigerator. Arrange the fish fillets on a grill basket in your Air fryer oven.

2. Air Frying. Bake at 330 degrees for 8 to 9 minutes, or until salmon fillets are easily flaked with a fork. Work with batches and serve warm.

Nutrition:

Energy (calories): 140 kcal

Protein: 2.47 g

Fat: 8.83 g

Carbohydrates: 13.39 g

40. Old Bay Crab Cakes

Preparation Time: 10 minutes

Cooking Time: 20 minutes

Servings: 4

Ingredients

- Two slices dried bread, crusts removed

- A small amount of milk

- 1 tbsp. mayonnaise

- 1 tbsp. Worcestershire sauce

- 1 tbsp. baking powder

- 1 tbsp. parsley flakes

- 1 tsp. Old Bay® Seasoning

- 1/4 tsp. salt

- One egg

- 1 pound lump crabmeat

Directions:

1. Preparing the **Ingredients**. Crush your bread over a large bowl until it is broken down into small pieces. Add milk and stir until bread crumbs are moistened. Mix in mayo and

Worcestershire sauce. Add remaining ingredients and mix well. Shape into four patties.

2. Air Frying. Cook at 360 degrees for 20 minutes, flipping halfway through.

Nutrition:

Calories: 165

Carbs: 5.8g

Fat: 4.5g

Protein: 24g

Fiber: 0g

41. Scallops and Spring Veggies

Preparation Time: 10 minutes

Cooking Time: 8 minutes

Servings: 4

Ingredients

- ½ pound asparagus ends trimmed, cut into 2-inch pieces
- 1cup sugar snap peas
- 1 pound sea scallops
- 1 tbsp. lemon juice
- 2 tsp. olive oil
- ½ tsp. dried thyme
- Pinch salt
- Freshly ground black pepper

Directions:

1. Preparing the **Ingredients**. In the Oven Rack/Basket, put the asparagus and sugar snap peas. Place the rack on the Air Fryer Oven's middle shelf.

2. Air Frying. Cook for 2 to 3 minutes or until the vegetables are just starting to get tender.

3. Meanwhile, check the scallops for a small muscle attached to the side, and pull it off and discard.

4. In a prepared medium bowl, toss the scallops with lemon juice, olive oil, thyme, salt, and pepper. Place into the Oven rack/basket on top of the vegetables. Place the rack on the Air Fryer Oven's middle shelf.

5. Air Frying. Set temperature to 360°F. Steam for 5 to 7 minutes. Until the scallops are just firm and the vegetables are tender. Serve immediately.

Nutrition:

Calories: 162

Carbs: 10g

Fat: 4g

Protein: 22g

Fiber: 3g

42. Fried Calamari

Preparation Time: 8 minutes

Cooking Time: 7 minutes

Servings: 6-8

Ingredients

- ½ tsp. salt ½ tsp. Old Bay seasoning

- 1/3 C. plain cornmeal ½ C. semolina flour

- ½ C. almond flour 5-6 C. olive oil

- 1½ pounds baby squid

Directions:

1. Preparing the **Ingredients**. Rinse squid in cold water and slice tentacles, keeping just ¼-inch of the hood in one piece.

2. Combine 1-2 pinches of pepper, salt, Old Bay seasoning, cornmeal, and both flours. Dredge squid pieces into flour mixture and place into the Air fryer oven.

3. Air Frying. Spray liberally with olive oil. Cook 15 minutes at 345 degrees till the coating turns a golden brown.

Nutrition:

Calories: 211 Carbs: 55g Fat: 6g Protein: 21g

Sugar: 1g

43. Soy and Ginger Shrimp

Preparation Time: 8 minutes

Cooking Time: 10 minutes

Servings: 4

Ingredients

- 2tbsps. olive oil

- 2 tbsps. scallions, finely chopped

- Two cloves garlic, chopped

- 1 tsp. fresh ginger, grated

- 1 tbsp. dry white wine

- 1 tbsp. balsamic vinegar

- 1/4 cup soy sauce

- 1 tbsp. sugar

- 1 pound shrimp

- Salt and ground black pepper to taste

Directions:

1. Preparing the **Ingredients**. To make the marinade, warm the oil in a saucepan; cook all ingredients, except the shrimp, salt, and black pepper. Now, let it cool.

2. Marinate the shrimp, covered, at least an hour, in the refrigerator.

3. Air Frying. After that, bake the shrimp at 350 degrees F for 8 to 10 minutes (depending on the size) turning once or twice. Season prepared shrimp with salt and black pepper and serve right away.

Nutrition:

Energy (calories): 239 kcal

Protein: 24.7 g

Fat: 11.22 g

Carbohydrates: 8.51 g

CHAPTER 8:

Bakery and Desserts

44. Air-Fried S'mores

Preparation Time: 10 minutes

Cooking Time: 10 minutes

Servings: 4

Ingredients:

- Whole graham crackers (4)

- Marshmallows (2)

- Chocolate - such as Hershey's (4 pieces)

Directions:

1. Break the graham crackers in half to make eight squares. Cut the marshmallows in half crosswise with a pair of scissors.

2. Place the marshmallows cut side down on four graham squares. Place marshmallow side up in the basket of the Air

Fryer and cook at 390° Fahrenheit for four to five minutes, or until golden.

3. Remove them from the fryer and place a piece Break all graham crackers in half to create eight squares. Cut marshmallows in half crosswise.

4. Place the marshmallows, cut side down, on four graham squares of chocolate and graham square on top of each toasted marshmallow and serve.

Nutrition:

Calories 111

Fats 8g

Protein 4 g

45. Apple Chips

Preparation Time: 10 minutes

Cooking Time: 5 minutes

Servings: 2

Ingredients:

- Cinnamon (.5 tsp.)
- Apple (1)
- Sugar (1 tbsp.)
- Pinch kosher salt (1 pinch)

Directions:

1. Warm the Air Fryer in advance to reach 390° Fahrenheit.
2. Slice the apples lengthwise and arrange them in a dish with cinnamon, sugar, and salt. Toss.
3. Cook them until they are crispy or around seven to eight minutes. Turn halfway through the cycle.
4. Transfer to a platter and serve.

Nutrition:

Calories 107

Fats 6g Protein 5g

46. Banana S'mores

Preparation Time: 10 minutes **Cooking Time:** 5 minutes

Servings: 4

Ingredients:

- Bananas (4) Mini-peanut butter chips (3 tbsp.)

- Graham cracker cereal (3 tbsp.)

- Mini-chocolate chips - semi-sweet (3 tbsp.)

Directions:

1. Heat the Air Fryer in advance at 400° Fahrenheit.

2. Slice the un-peeled bananas lengthwise along the inside of the curve. Don't slice through the bottom. Open slightly - forming a pocket.

3. Fill each pocket with chocolate chips, peanut butter chips, and marshmallows. Poke the cereal into the filling.

4. Arrange the stuffed bananas in the fryer basket, keeping them upright with the filling facing up.

5. Air-fry until the peel has blackened about 6 minutes.

6. Chill for 1-2 minutes. Spoon out the filling to serve.

Nutrition: Calories 97 Fats 10 g Protein 9g

47. Cherry Pie

Preparation Time: 10 minutes

Cooking Time: 15 minutes

Servings: 8

Ingredients:

- Cherry pie filling (21 oz. can) Milk (1 tbsp.)

- Refrigerated pie crusts (2) Egg yolk (1)

Directions:

1. Warm the fryer at 310° Fahrenheit.

2. Poke holes into the crust after placing it in a pie plate. Allow the excess to hang over the edges. Place in the Air Fryer for 5 minutes

3. Transfer the basket with the pie plate onto the countertop. Fill it with cherries. Remove the excess crust.

4. Cut the remaining crust into ¾-inch strips - weaving a lattice across the pie.

5. Make an egg wash using the milk and egg. Brush the pie. Air-fry for 15 minutes. Serve with a scoop of ice cream.

Nutrition: Calories 109 Fats 12 g Protein 8 g

48. Fluffy Peanut Butter Marshmallow Turnovers

Preparation Time: 5 minutes

Cooking Time: 20 minutes

Servings: 4

Ingredients:

- Filo pastry (4 defrosted sheets)

- Chunky peanut butter (4 tbsp.)

- Melted butter (2 oz.)

- Marshmallow fluff (4 tsp.)

- Sea salt (1 pinch)

Directions:

1. Set the temperature of the Air Fryer at 360° Fahrenheit.

2. Use the melted butter to brush one sheet of the filo. Put the second sheet on top and brush it also with butter. Continue the process until you have completed all four sheets.

3. Cut the layers into four—12-inch x 3-inch strips.

4. Place one tsp. of the marshmallow fluff on the underside and one tbsp. of the peanut butter.

5. Fold the tip over the filo strip to form a triangle, making sure the filling is completely wrapped.

6. Seal the ends with a small amount of butter. Place the completed turnovers into the Air Fryer for three to five minutes.

7. When done, they will be fluffy and golden brown.

8. Add a touch of sea salt for the sweet/salty combo. Serve.

Nutrition:

Calories 120

Fats 13g

Protein 9g

49. Funnel Cake Bites

Preparation Time: 10 minutes

Cooking Time: 20 minutes

Servings: 8

Ingredients:

- Greek yogurt (1 cup)

- Self-rising flour (1 cup - divided)

- For Dusting: Powdered sugar

- Optional: Vanilla bean paste (1 tbsp.)

Directions:

1. Heat the Air Fryer at 375° Fahrenheit.

2. Combine the yogurt, ¾ of the flour, and vanilla if using.

3. Roll out the dough using the remainder of the flour.

4. Slice it into 32 squares and place in the Air Fryer (8 at a time).

5. Set the timer for 4 minutes. Flip then over and continue to air-fry for another 3 to 4 minutes until ready.

6. Lightly dust with the sugar as desired and serve.

Nutrition: Calories 107 Fats 9g Protein 6g

50. Healthy Pop-Tarts

Preparation Time: 10 minutes

Cooking Time: 15 minutes

Servings: 6

Ingredients:

- Strawberries (.33 cup or 8 oz. - quartered)

- Granulated sugar (.25 cup)

- Refrigerated pie crusts (14.1 oz. pkg. Use 1)

- Powdered sugar (.t cup/2 oz.)

- Lemon juice (1.5 tsp./1 lemon)

Directions:

1. Stir the strawberries and granulated sugar in a medium-sized microwavable bowl. Let the mixture stand for 15 minutes, stirring occasionally. Microwave on high until shiny and reduced, about 10 minutes, stirring halfway through cooking. Cool completely, about 30 minutes.

2. Roll the pie crust into a 12-inch circle on a lightly floured surface. Cut the dough into 12 rectangles (2.5 x 3-inch), rerolling scraps, as needed.

3. Spoon about two tsp. strawberry mixture into the center of six of the dough rectangles, leaving a .5-inch border. Brush the edges of filled dough rectangles with water, top with remaining dough rectangles, pressing edges with a fork to seal. Coat tarts well with a cooking oil spray.

4. Place three tarts in a single layer in the Air Fryer basket, and cook at 350° Fahrenheit or until it's golden brown (10 min.). Repeat with remaining tarts.

5. Place on a wire rack to cool completely, about 30 minutes.

6. Whisk the powdered sugar and lemon juice in a small bowl until smooth. Spoon the glaze over cooled tarts.

7. If you want, add a few candy sprinkles.

Nutrition:

Calories 109

Fats 10g

Protein 5g

Conclusion

I hope this Air Fryer Toaster Oven Cookbook allows you to understand this groundbreaking kitchen appliance's dynamics and principles, why you should use it, and how it's going to change your outlook on food preparation, creative cooking, and healthier lifestyles. The Air fryer Toaster Oven has all the benefits of a toaster oven, with the powerful air frying technology of an air fryer. The air fryer toaster oven will make you forget your old toaster oven. The controls are easy, intuitive and on display, like the air fryer. You don't need to worry about a frying pan clean-up either. The heavy "chicken" bottom cavity of the toaster oven can also get hot enough to cook your food in a short amount of time. An air fryer is the perfect kitchen appliance for toaster oven people. Now you can cook your bread, pizza, chicken, meat and fish, store in air fryer toaster oven without oils for long-lasting taste.

I encourage you to share these recipes with family and friends, tell them about this cookbook, and let them know about Air fryer toaster oven's benefits. This cookbook will prepare you to obtain the ultimate in performance and convenience by taking full advantage of the power-to-weight ratio of this versatile appliance. Now you can get the maximum benefits of this cookbook and make it last a lifetime with excellent food and wonderful health. Let this book be a guide to your success and let this cookbook become an inspiration to give your family healthy food in a more convenient and creative way. Let your family prepare their meals in a more creative and tasty way in every aspect. Let the benefits of this cookbook make you more aware of and more open to food and a healthy lifestyle. The quality of life depends upon the quality of food you eat.

As you enjoy more and more delicious and healthy food coming out of the kitchen, start looking forward to a highly satisfying experience with your new air fryer toaster oven. Get motivated as you prepare for healthy and delicious food that makes taste so much better without the deep flavors and the sharp tastes of so-called 'healthy meals'.

CPSIA information can be obtained
at www.ICGtesting.com
Printed in the USA
LVHW022114110521
687091LV00012B/2575